AF352049

Air Fryer Cookbook

Easy, Delicious, and Healthy Air Fryer Recipes for Busy People

Savannah Gibbs

Table of Contents

Introduction

Do you like the taste and texture of fried chicken, french fries, and onion rings? You might be concerned that traditionally fried foods are laden with oil and calories. What if you could eat healthy and still enjoy your favorite fried dishes? You can with an air fryer. With its Rapid Air technology, the air fryer is the perfect solution for preparing healthy, crispy, and tender meals or snacks, using little or no oil.

The versatility and functionality of the air fryer is unbelievable. This book will show you how an air fryer works, what the benefits of using it are, and how to maximize its use. It also provides 42 easy and delicious air fryer recipes, some taking as little as a few minutes to prepare.

Thank you for purchasing this book!

CHAPTER ONE

Air Fryer 101

Air fryers were first introduced in Europe and Australia in 2010, followed by Japan and North America. Over the years, this appliance has become a staple in today's kitchen, providing a new and healthy way of preparing foods. It is used in different ways in different countries: the Japanese use air fryers to make fried prawns; Americans use it to prepare chicken wings; and Indians use it to make samosas!

You may have watched numerous advertisements for air fryers and probably wondered how it works. If you associate an air fryer with a lot of hot air, then you have the right idea. An air fryer uses Rapid Air technology to cook foods with little oil. Foods are placed in the fryer's basket, and hot air is circulated rapidly around the ingredients. The air helps to heat the food from all sides at once, which is exactly what happens when you deep fry foods using oil. The air fryer uses 90 percent less oil, and won't leave your kitchen with a greasy smell. This technology also ensures an optimal temperature is maintained within the fryer to avoid burning your food. The air fryer will make your food crispy on the outside and tender and tasty on the inside!

Benefits of Air Fryers

When you look at a new kitchen appliance, you want to know the benefits of using it before splurging on the purchase. Let's look at a few benefits of the air fryer, which may give you a clearer idea as to whether or not you should consider getting it for your kitchen.

Low Fat Air Frying

Let's be honest, it's hard to deny that fried food tastes good. We all love it. The air fryer lets you enjoy that decadent fried taste with only a spoonful of oil. You'll save calories, lose weight, and get healthier while still enjoying crispy french fries and fried chicken. The tray below the air fryer ends up collecting all the excess fat that would normally end up in your body when using traditional frying methods.

Faster

The hot air prepares food quickly, so it saves you time. After a long day at work, the last thing you want to do is spend your precious time in front of the stove. The air fryer cooks your favorite meals in minutes.

Simple to Use

There aren't a lot of buttons on the air fryer to confuse you. You only have to set the timer and temperature, and wait for the food to be prepared. There are some fryers that come with additional buttons to indicate what kind of ingredient is being cooked, making it easier for you.

This is an appliance that a person with little to no cooking knowledge or experience can use. All you will need to do is put the ingredients in the basket and set the temperature and the timer without worrying about another thing–the machine will do the rest of the work.

Safe

This appliance is extremely safe to use. It automatically turns off when the food finishes cooking, which prevents overheating the appliance and the food from being burnt. Your children can also use this appliance–you do not have to worry about them burning themselves when cooking since the fryer is essentially oil-free and covered.

Easy to Clean

All the parts of the air fryer can be removed easily and are dishwasher friendly. If you do not own a dishwasher, you can soak the parts in water and clean them with a sponge, which is easier than having to clean multiple utensils you may have to use when cooking with oil.

CHAPTER TWO

Using and Caring for an Air Fryer

When you use an air fryer for the first time, you may make a few mistakes that could eventually ruin the appliance. This chapter provides a few tips to keep in mind when you start using an air fryer.

Always Shake and Mix

When you cook using oil, it helps to mix your food properly, which cooks every little piece in the skillet or pan on all sides. This does not happen in an air fryer, since the air is not strong enough to separate the ingredients. To avoid undercooked food, you will need to open the machine at least once to shake the ingredients in the basket while cooking. Most people remove the basket halfway through the cooking to shake the ingredients. For example, if you were to set a timer for twenty minutes, you would need to pause the fryer after ten minutes and mix the ingredients before you restart the fryer again.

Keep it Light

One mistake most people make when using the air fryer is that they overcrowd it. When you deep-fry food, you know the quantity of food that needs to be cooked in the oil, but when you use an air fryer, you may not leave enough space for the ingredients to cook properly. If you ever hear of people complaining about how their air fryer doesn't make their food crispy, then they are probably making this mistake. Read the manual carefully to ensure you do not overload the basket.

Use Cooking Spray

Although the air fryer manual says you don't need to add oil, you may need to use a tablespoon of oil to ensure your food has the best taste. If you do not want to use oil, you can use cooking spray, otherwise, your food may stick to the fryer's surface.

Start with Room Temperature

When you cook using fresh ingredients, do not start cooking them immediately after you take them out of the fridge. Let the ingredients warm to room temperature before placing them in the fryer. This will reduce the cooking time and will also give you crispier results.

Do More with It

Although this appliance is called an air "fryer", it does a lot more than just fry food. You can make anything from noodles to a pizza in an air fryer. An air fryer has more in common with a fan-forced oven rather than a deep fryer. You can roast, bake, and grill in an air fryer. In other words, experiment!

Take Good Care

To take good care of your air fryer, you don't have to clean it constantly, but like every other electronic appliance, it does need a certain level of care. If you use your air fryer regularly, you will need to clean it every five to 10 days to prevent unwanted smells. Use a dishwasher to clean the removable parts of the fryer or soak them in soapy water before cleaning them gently with a sponge.

CHAPTER THREE

Air Fryer Breakfast Recipes

Breakfast Burrito

Yield: 2 servings
Preparation Time: 10 minutes
Cooking Time: 8 minutes
Total Time: 18 minutes
Ingredients:
2 large eggs
4 thin slices turkey or chicken (white meat)
4 tablespoons diced bell pepper
6 thin avocado slices
3 tablespoons grated mozzarella
2 tortillas
3 tablespoons salsa
Salt and pepper to taste

Directions:
1. Preheat air fryer to 360 degrees F.
2. Whisk the eggs in a bowl and add the salt and pepper.
3. Place a small pan inside the basket of the air fryer. Spray the pan with a non-stick cooking spray.
4. Pour the eggs into the pan and cook for 5 minutes.
5. Carefully remove the pan from the air fryer.
6. Fill the tortillas with equal amounts of egg, turkey or chicken, pepper, avocado, grated cheese, and salsa. Be careful not to overstuff the tortillas.
7. Roll and firmly wrap the tortillas.
8. Place the tortillas on a tray in the air fryer.

9. Decrease the heat to 350 degrees F and cook for 3 minutes.

10. Serve hot, with salsa on the side.

Cheese Omelet

Yield: 1 serving

Preparation Time: 5 minutes

Cooking Time: 15 minutes

Total Time: 20 minutes

Ingredients:

2 large eggs

1 onion, diced

$\frac{1}{8}$ teaspoon hot sauce

$\frac{1}{4}$ cup cheddar cheese, grated

Salt and pepper to taste

Directions:

1. Preheat the air fryer to 360 degrees F.

2. In a bowl, whisk the eggs until fluffy and stir in the hot sauce, salt, and pepper.

3. Place a small pan inside the air fryer and spray with a non-stick cooking spray.

4. Put the onions in the pan and cook for 10 minutes.

5. Pour the whisked eggs over the onions and top with the cheddar cheese.

6. Cook the omelet for another 5 minutes.

Spring Rolls

Yield: 4 servings
Preparation Time: 15 minutes
Cooking Time: 5 minutes
Total Time: 20 minutes
Ingredients:
For the Filling:
4 ounces cooked chicken breast, pulled
1 celery stalk, thinly sliced
1 medium carrot, thinly sliced
½ cup mushrooms, thinly sliced
½ teaspoon ginger, minced
1 teaspoon brown sugar
1 teaspoon chicken stock powder
Salt and pepper to taste
For the Wrappers:
1 egg, beaten
1 teaspoon cornstarch
8 spring roll wrappers
½ teaspoon vegetable oil

Directions:
1. Preheat air fryer to 390 degrees F.
2. Add chicken, celery, carrot, mushrooms, ginger, sugar, and chicken stock to a bowl and mix until well combined.
3. Add in salt and pepper to taste.
4. Place a wrapper on a plate and add 1 tbsp. of the filling.
5. In a bowl, mix the cornstarch and egg together. Use the egg mixture to line the sides of the wrapper. Roll into a spring roll.
6. Apply oil to top of each roll and place them in the basket.
7. Fry for 3 to 4 minutes at 360 degrees F or until golden on the outside.
8. Serve with a sauce of your choice.

Blueberry Muffins

Yield: 5–6 servings
Preparation Time: 10 minutes
Cooking Time: 10 minutes
Total Time: 20 minutes
Ingredients:
1 cup blueberries
1½ cups flour
1/3 cup white sugar
2 teaspoons baking powder
½ teaspoon salt
1 large egg
1 cup plain yogurt
1/3 cup canola oil
2 teaspoons vanilla
2 tablespoons brown sugar

Directions:
1. Wash and place blueberries in a bowl and coat thoroughly with one tablespoon of the flour.

2. In another bowl, mix remaining flour, sugar, baking powder, and salt. Stir well to combine.

3. In a third bowl, whisk the egg, yogurt, and oil. Stir in vanilla.

4. Add the egg mixture to dry ingredients and stir well.

5. Fold the blueberries into batter.

6. Place 5–6 muffin cups inside air fryer basket.

7. Pour batter equally among muffin cups.

8. Sprinkle dash of brown sugar on top of each muffin.

9. Heat the air fryer to 360 degrees F and cook for 10 minutes.

10. Check for doneness by sticking a toothpick in the center of a muffin. Toothpick should come out clean.

11. If necessary, cook another 2 minutes.

Quick Breakfast Frittata

Yield: 10 servings
Preparation Time: 5 minutes
Cooking Time: 12 minutes
Total Time: 17 minutes
Ingredients:
4 cherry tomatoes, halved
1 cup sausage, crumbled
4 large eggs
1 tablespoon olive oil
4 tablespoons chopped fresh parsley
½ cup parmesan cheese, grated
Salt and pepper to taste

Directions:
1. Preheat the air fryer to 390 degrees F.
2. Insert a small pan and put the cherry tomatoes and crumbled sausage in the pan.
3. Cook for 6–7 minutes.
4. In a bowl, whisk together the eggs, parsley, cheese, salt, and pepper.
5. Pour the egg mixture over the tomatoes and sausage.
6. Bake in the air fryer for 5–6 more minutes.

Fried Tofu

Yield: 4 servings
Preparation Time: 5 minutes
Cooking Time: 20 minutes
Total Time: 25 minutes
Ingredients:
1 block of tofu, chopped into cubes
2 tablespoons cornstarch
¼ cup rice flour
Salt and pepper to taste
2 tablespoons olive oil

Directions:
1. Preheat air fryer to 390 degrees F.
2. Add cornstarch, rice flour, salt, pepper, and oil to a bowl and mix until well combined.
3. Add tofu cubes and coat them thoroughly.
4. Add to the basket and fry for 15 to 20 minutes or until crispy.
5. Serve hot, with a sauce of your choice.

Baked Eggs and Tomatoes

Yield: 2 servings
Preparation Time: 5 minutes
Cooking Time: 10 minutes
Total Time: 15 minutes
Ingredients:
1 sliced tomato
2 eggs
2 tablespoons whole milk or cream
3 tablespoons grated cheddar cheese
Salt and pepper to taste
Optional: 1 teaspoon of your favorite herbs

Directions:
1. Heat the air fryer to 360 degrees F.
2. Divide the sliced tomato between 2 ramekins.
3. Add the salt and pepper, and any herbs of your choice.
4. In a bowl, whisk the eggs and milk together.
5. Transfer the egg mixture to the 2 ramekins. Top with the grated cheese.
6. Place the ramekins in the basket of the air fryer. Cook for 10 minutes.
7. Serve with hot sauce, sour cream, or salsa.

Cauliflower Fritters

Yield: 6 servings
Preparation Time: 10 minutes
Cooking Time: 25 minutes
Total Time: 35 minutes
Ingredients:
1 large cauliflower
1 tablespoon chili powder
½ teaspoon turmeric powder
Salt to taste
2 tablespoons vegetable oil

Directions:
1. Boil the cauliflower and separate it into florets.
2. Add it to a bowl along with chili powder, turmeric, and salt, and mix until well combined. Allow it to stand for 10 minutes.
3. Preheat air fryer to 390 degrees F.
4. Brush oil over the cauliflower and add to the basket.
5. Fry for 10 to 15 minutes or until crispy.
6. Serve hot, with a sauce of your choice.

CHAPTER FOUR
Air Fryer Lunch Recipes

Vegetable Salad with Vinaigrette

Yield: 6 servings
Preparation Time: 20 minutes
Cooking Time: 20 minutes
Total Time: 40 minutes
Ingredients:
1 white cauliflower, chopped into florets
1 purple cauliflower, chopped into florets
3 beets, peeled and chopped into bite-size pieces
1 teaspoon olive oil
4 cups endives, chopped
1 cup arugula, chopped
6 radishes, sliced
½ cup mint, chopped

For the Vinaigrette:
½ cup parsley
½ cup cilantro
¼ cup chives
1 shallot, minced
1 garlic clove, minced
3 tablespoons lemon juice
1/3 cup red wine vinegar
½ cup olive oil
Salt and pepper to taste

Directions:
1. Preheat the air fryer to 360 degrees F.

2. Place the cauliflower in a bowl, and coat with a little olive oil.

3. In another bowl, add the beets, and coat with a little olive oil.

4. Add the cauliflower to the basket of the air fryer. Cook for 8 minutes and transfer to a plate.

5. Place the beets in the fry basket and cook for 12 minutes. Transfer to a plate.

6. For the vinaigrette, put the parsley, cilantro, chives, shallot, garlic, lemon juice, and vinegar in a blender. Puree ingredients while slowly adding the olive oil.

7. Toss the cauliflower and beets in a large bowl.

8. Add the endive and arugula. Pour the vinaigrette over the salad.

9. Garnish the salad with the radishes and mint.

Cheeseburger with Everything

Yield: 2 servings
Preparation Time: 5 minutes
Cooking Time: 11 minutes
Total Time: 16 minutes
Ingredients:
1 lb. ground beef
2 slices Swiss or American cheese
4 bacon strips (optional)
2 hamburger buns
4 onion slices
4 tomato slices
Lettuce leaves
Condiments

Directions:
1. Heat the air fryer to 360 degrees F.
2. Shape the ground beef into 2 patties.
3. Place patties and the bacon into the basket of the air fryer. Cook for 8 minutes.
4. Top the hamburger patties with cheese and onions.
5. Place the sliced buns on top of the burgers.
6. Continue cooking for 3 minutes.
7. Add tomato slices, lettuce, and desired condiments.

Vegetable Dumplings

Yield: 5 servings
Preparation Time: 10 minutes
Cooking Time: 35 minutes
Total Time: 45 minutes
Ingredients:
For the Stuffing:
2 cups cabbage, shredded
1 carrot, chopped
2 large onions, chopped
1 green pepper
1 2-inch slice ginger
8 garlic cloves, chopped
Salt and pepper to taste
1 tablespoon soy sauce
1 tablespoon olive oil
1 scallion

For the Rolls:
10 spring roll sheets
2 tablespoons corn flour or plain flour
Water

Directions:
1. Preheat air fryer to 390 degrees F.
2. Add oil to a pan along with onions and garlic and sauté.
3. Add green pepper, cabbage, and ginger and sauté till brown.
4. Add salt, pepper, and soy sauce and mix until well combined.
5. Add scallion last and mix.
6. Lay spring roll sheet on a plate and add about 2 tablespoons of filling.

7. Make a paste using flour and water. Use a finger to apply the paste on the edges of the spring roll sheet. Roll sheet to seal the filling in.

8. Add to fryer and fry for 20 minutes or until crispy.

9. Serve warm, with noodles and a sauce of your choice.

Fried Chicken Sandwich

Yield: 2 servings
Preparation Time: 5 minutes
Cooking Time: 7 minutes
Total Time: 12 minutes
Ingredients:
2 chicken breasts, boneless and skinless
2 large eggs
½ cup whole milk
1 cup flour
2 tablespoons sugar
½ teaspoon garlic powder
2 tablespoons olive oil
2 hamburger buns
Salt and pepper to taste

Directions:
1. Heat the air fry to 350 degrees F.

2. Place the chicken breasts in a plastic bag and use a mallet to pound the meat to a ½-inch thickness.

3. Cut the chicken into several large pieces.

4. Whisk the eggs and milk in a bowl.

5. In another bowl, stir the flour with the sugar, garlic powder, salt, and pepper.

6. Dip the chicken pieces in the egg mixture, then coat them with the flour mixture.

7. Spray the bottom of the air fryer with a non-stick cooking spray. Cook chicken for 5 minutes.

8. Flip the chicken and cook another 6 minutes.

9. Increase the heat to 390 degrees F and cook 2 more minutes.

10. Toast the hamburger buns and assemble the sandwiches.

11. If desired, add mayonnaise and pickles.

Asian Steak

Yield: 4 servings
Preparation Time: 2 hours
Cooking Time: 15 minutes
Total Time: 2 hours 15 minutes
Ingredients:
1 pound steak
1 cup cilantro leaves, finely chopped
¼ cup mint leaves, finely chopped
2 tablespoons oregano leaves, finely chopped
3 garlic cloves, finely chopped
1 teaspoon red pepper powder
1 tablespoon cumin powder
1 teaspoon cayenne pepper powder
2 teaspoon smoked paprika powder
Salt to taste
¼ teaspoon black pepper
1 tablespoon olive oil
3 tablespoons red wine vinegar

Directions:
1. Add cilantro leaves, mint leaves, oregano leaves, cloves, pepper powder, cumin powder, cayenne pepper, paprika, salt, and pepper to a bowl along with oil and vinegar, and mix until well combined.

2. Cut steak into small pieces. Add steak to herb mixture and marinate for 2 to 24 hours in fridge.

3. Preheat air fryer to 390 degrees F.

4. Pat steak dry using tissues. Place in basket and fry for 10 to 12 minutes or until desired doneness.

5. Serve with sauce of your choice.

Asparagus Salad

Yield: 4 servings
Preparation Time: 10 minutes
Cooking Time: 10 minutes
Total Time: 20 minutes
Ingredients:

10 oz. white asparagus

8 oz. green asparagus

1 cup chicory

4 boiled eggs

10 oz. boiled potatoes

10 oz. ham, cubed

6 small radishes, sliced

6 cherry tomatoes, halved

Lettuce leaves

1 tablespoon olive oil

Directions:

1. Remove the stems from the asparagus and cut into bite-sized pieces.

2. Insert a dish in the air fryer.

3. Preheat to 380 degrees F and add the olive oil.

4. Add asparagus, ham, and potatoes and cook for 10 minutes.

5. Remove the dish from the air fryer and let cool.

6. Stir in the radishes and tomatoes. Add salt and pepper to taste.

7. Chop the eggs and add to asparagus mix.

8. Lay the lettuce and chicory on a large plate and top with the asparagus mix. Serve warm.

Tuna Patties

Yield: 4 servings
Preparation Time: 10 minutes
Cooking Time: 10 minutes
Total Time: 20 minutes
Ingredients:
2 cans tuna in water
1 teaspoon Dijon mustard
½ cup panko breadcrumbs
2 tablespoons chopped parsley
1 tablespoon lemon juice
Dash of Tabasco or hot sauce
1 large egg
Salt and pepper to taste.

Directions:
1. Drain the liquid from the tuna and flake with a fork.
2. In a bowl, combine the tuna, mustard, breadcrumbs, parsley, lemon juice, and Tabasco sauce.
3. Add the egg and season with salt and pepper. Mix thoroughly.
4. Form 8 patties and refrigerate them overnight.
5. Preheat the air fryer to 360 degrees F.
6. Place the patties in the air fryer, spray with a non-stick cooking spray, and cook for 10 minutes. (For extra crispiness, cook an extra 3–4 minutes.)
7. Drizzle patties with lemon juice and serve.

Roasted Vegetables

Yield: 4 servings
Preparation Time: 5 minutes
Cooking Time: 10 minutes
Total Time: 15 minutes
Ingredients:
1 cup potato, chopped
1 cup celery stalks, chopped
2 red onions, chopped
1 butternut squash, chopped
1 tablespoon fresh thyme leaves
1 tablespoon olive oil
Salt and pepper to taste

Directions:
1. Preheat air fryer to 390 degrees F.
2. Add potatoes, celery, onion, squash, pepper, salt, and thyme to a bowl and mix until well combined.
3. Add in oil and toss.
4. Add vegetables to basket and fry for 10 minutes.
5. Serve hot.

CHAPTER FIVE

Air Fryer Snacks

Sweet Potato Fries

Yield: 6 servings
Preparation Time: 10 minutes
Cooking Time: 25 minutes
Total Time: 35 minutes
Ingredients:
1 lb. sweet potatoes
1 tablespoon vegetable oil

Directions:
1. Preheat air fryer to 340 degrees F.
2. Peel and cut potatoes into fries and place in a bowl.
3. Toss fries with the oil. It's okay to use your hands.
4. Add fries to basket and cook for approximately 15 min.
5. Shake basket to distribute the fries in the basket. Cook at 360 degrees F for 5 more minutes.
6. Shake basket and cook another 5 minutes.

Fried Dough with Amaretto Sauce

Yield: 20 servings
Preparation Time: 10 minutes
Cooking Time: 8 minutes
Total Time: 18 minutes
Ingredients:
1 lb. bread or pizza dough
½ cup melted, unsalted butter
½ cup sugar
1 cup heavy cream
12 oz. semi-sweet chocolate chips
2 tablespoons amaretto liqueur

Directions:
1. Roll out dough and form a log.
2. Cut the log into 20 pieces.
3. Halve each piece and twist the two halves together a few times to create a cork screw effect.
4. Place the dough slices on a baking sheet, brush with the melted butter, and top with the sugar.
5. Preheat the air fryer to 350 degrees F and brush a little melted butter on bottom of the basket.
6. In batches, air fry the dough for 5 minutes.
7. Turn the pieces over, brush the other sides with more butter and air fry another 3 minutes.
8. For the amaretto sauce, place the chocolate chips in a bowl.
9. Simmer the heavy cream in a pan until heated thoroughly. Pour the heavy cream over the chocolate chips and whisk until smooth. Add the amaretto liqueur.
10. Coat the air fried dough pieces with more sugar and serve with the sauce.

Cheddar Croquettes with Bacon

Yield: 6 servings
Preparation Time: 8 minutes
Cooking Time: 8 minutes
Total Time: 16 minutes
Ingredients:
1 lb. sharp cheddar cheese
½ lb. bacon
1 tablespoons olive oil
½ cup panko breadcrumbs
1 cup flour
2 eggs, beaten

Directions:
1. Slice cheddar cheese into 1-inch pieces.
2. Wrap a bacon slice around each piece. Place in freezer for 10 minutes.
3. Preheat the air fryer to 370 degrees F.
4. Combine the olive oil and breadcrumbs.
5. In separate dishes place the flour, the breadcrumbs, and the eggs.
6. Coat the cheese with the flour, then dip in the eggs, and press into the breadcrumbs.
7. Transfer the croquettes to the cooking basket and cook for approximately 8 minutes, or until golden brown.

Crab Cakes

Yield: 10 servings
Preparation Time: 10 minutes
Cooking Time: 25 minutes
Total Time: 35 minutes
Ingredients:
4 cups crab meat
12 Ritz crackers
1 large egg
1 onion, chopped
1 scallion, chopped
1 tablespoon corn flour
1 tablespoon mayonnaise
½ teaspoon garlic powder
Salt and pepper to taste

Directions:
1. Mix all the ingredients together in a bowl and shape into 10 patties.
2. Preheat the air fryer to 360 degrees F.
3. Add crab cake patties to basket and cook for 10 minutes.

Old Fashioned Onion Rings

Yield: 4 servings
Preparation Time: 10 minutes
Cooking Time: 10 minutes
Total Time: 20 minutes
Ingredients:
1 cup flour
1½ teaspoons baking powder
1 teaspoon salt
1 onion, sliced
¾ cup milk
1 egg, beaten
¾ cup panko breadcrumbs

Directions:
1. Preheat the air fryer to 360 degrees F.
2. Mix together the flour, baking powder, and salt.
3. Coat each onion slice with the flour mixture.
4. Whisk together the milk and egg.
5. Dip each onion ring in the egg mixture.
6. In a shallow dish, press the onion rings into the breadcrumbs.
7. Transfer the battered onion rings to the air fryer; cook for approximately 10 minutes, or until brown.

Buffalo Wings

Yield: 4 servings
Preparation Time: 10 minutes
Cooking Time: 14 minutes
Total Time: 24 minutes
Ingredients:
2 lbs. chicken wings
3 tablespoons melted butter
6 tablespoons hot sauce
Salt and pepper to taste

Extra Sauce:
3 tablespoons melted butter
¼ cup hot sauce

Directions:
1. Cut the tips off the chicken wings.
2. Stir together the melted butter and the hot sauce.
3. Marinate the chicken wings in the hot sauce for several hours or overnight in the fridge.
4. Preheat air fryer to 390 degrees F.
5. Place the wings in the basket and cook for 14 minutes.
6. Prepare the extra sauce by mixing the butter and hot sauce.
7. Transfer the wings to a bowl or plastic bag and toss with extra sauce.
8. Serve with a ranch or blue cheese dip.

Coconut Shrimp

Yield: 4 servings
Preparation Time: 10 minutes
Cooking Time: 15 minutes
Total Time: 25 minutes
Ingredients:
1 lb. shrimp, peeled and deveined
½ cup flour
2 egg whites, beaten
½ cup panko breadcrumbs
½ cup coconut, shredded
1 teaspoon lime juice
½ teaspoon salt
Duck sauce

Directions:
1. Set 3 plates on the counter. Fill the plates respectively with the flour, eggs whites and breadcrumbs.
2. Blend the salt with the flour.
3. Beat the egg whites until stiff.
4. Blend the coconut and lime juice with the breadcrumbs.
5. Preheat air fryer to 390 degrees F.
6. Coat each shrimp with the flour, then dip in the egg whites, and then press into the breadcrumb mixture. Make sure all sides of the shrimps are coated.
7. Coat fryer basket with a non-stick cooking spray. Cook the shrimp in batches for 6 minutes.
8. When all the shrimp are fried, add all of them to the basket and cook at 350 degrees F for another 2 minutes.
9. Serve with duck sauce.

Roasted Carrots

Serves: 2

Preparation Time: 2 hours

Cooking Time: 15 minutes

Total Time: 2 hours 15 minutes

Ingredients:

1 cup carrots, split in half

Olive oil to brush

4 tablespoons honey

Salt and pepper to taste

Directions:

1. Add carrots to a bowl along with honey, oil, salt, and pepper and marinate for 2 to 3 hours.

2. Preheat air fryer to 390 degrees F.

3. Add carrots and fry for 10 to 12 minutes.

4. Serve warm.

CHAPTER SIX

Air Fryer Dinner Recipes

Buttermilk Chicken

Yield: 4–6 servings
Preparation Time: 10 minutes
Cooking Time: 10 minutes
Total Time: 20 minutes
Ingredients:
2 lbs. chicken thighs
Salt and pepper to taste
1 tablespoon garlic powder
1 tablespoon paprika
2 cups buttermilk
2 cups flour

Directions:
1. Wash chicken thighs thoroughly and pat dry.
2. In a bowl, mix together pepper, salt, garlic powder, and paprika.
3. Rub chicken pieces with the mixture and refrigerate overnight.
4. Preheat air fryer to 360 degrees F.
5. Dip chicken in the buttermilk, then coat with the flour.
6. Transfer chicken to fryer basket and set in one layer.
7. Cook for 10 minutes, turn chicken, and cook for another 10 minutes.

Chicken Cordon Bleu

Yield: 4 servings
Preparation Time: 5 minutes
Cooking Time: 8 minutes
Total Time: 13 minutes
Ingredients:
2 chicken breasts
1 tablespoon tarragon
Salt and pepper to taste
2 tablespoons cream cheese
1 teaspoon parsley
1 tablespoon garlic powder
2 slices Swiss cheese
2 slices cooked ham
1 large egg, beaten
¼ cup breadcrumbs

Directions:
1. Preheat the air fryer to 360 degrees F.
2. Season chicken with the tarragon, salt, and pepper.
3. Use a sharp knife to cut a slit in the middle of each breast.
4. Mix the cream cheese, parsley, and garlic powder, and spoon into the opening in each breast.
5. Cut the Swiss cheese slice and ham slices in two, and add 1 slice each to breasts.
6. Press in order to seal the opening and keep the stuffing inside.
7. With the beaten egg on one plate and the breadcrumbs in another, dip each breast into the beaten egg and then press into the breadcrumbs.
8. Transfer the chicken breasts to the air fryer.
9. Cook at 360 degrees F for 15 minutes.
10. Flip the chicken breasts over and cook for another 15 minutes.

Salmon with Dill Sauce

Yield: 4 servings
Preparation Time: 5 minutes
Cooking Time: 30 minutes
Total Time: 35 minutes
Ingredients:
For the Salmon:
2 salmon fillets
1 teaspoon olive oil
Salt to taste
For the Dill Sauce:
½ cup yogurt (non-fat)
¼ cup sour cream
Salt to taste
1 tablespoon dill, finely chopped

Directions:
1. Preheat air fryer to 250 degrees F.
2. Cut salmon into four portions. Pour a little olive oil onto each portion and sprinkle with salt.
3. Place seasoned salmon in basket and cook for 30 minutes.
4. While salmon is cooking, mix ingredients for dill sauce in a bowl.
5. When salmon is fully cooked, top salmon with sauce and serve warm.

Chicken Tandoori

Yield: 4 servings
Preparation Time: 5 minutes
Cooking Time: 15 minutes
Total Time: 20 minutes
Ingredients:
4 chicken thighs
Salt and pepper to taste
½ teaspoon chili paste
½ teaspoon garlic paste
¼ teaspoon garam masala powder
¼ teaspoon coriander
¼ teaspoon cumin
1 teaspoon lime juice
2 tablespoon Greek yogurt
1 teaspoon olive oil

Directions:
1. Use a sharp knife to score the chicken thighs in several places.
2. Combine all other ingredients except for the olive oil in a bowl.
3. Thoroughly coat the chicken with the spice mix and refrigerate for a few hours.
4. Preheat the air fryer to 380 degrees F.
5. Add the chicken thighs and cook for 10 minutes.
6. Remove the chicken from the basket and brush with the olive oil.
7. Return chicken to the air fryer and cook for 5 more minutes.
8. Serve with rice.

Pork Chops

Yield: 2 servings
Preparation Time: 10 minutes
Cooking Time: 10 minutes
Total Time: 20 minutes
Ingredients:
2 pork chops
Salt and pepper to taste
1/3 cup flour
1 large egg, beaten
½ cup panko breadcrumbs
1 tablespoon olive oil

Directions:
1. Preheat air fryer to 350 degrees F.
2. Season the pork chops with salt and pepper.
3. Place the flour, egg, and breadcrumbs in three separate shallow bowls.
4. Coat the chops with the flour, then dip in the egg, and then press into the crumbs.
5. Drizzle a little oil over the chops.
6. Place pork chops in the air fryer, and cook for 12 minutes.

Middle Eastern Meatballs

Yield: 6 servings
Preparation Time: 15 minutes
Cooking Time: 8 minutes
Total Time: 23 minutes
Ingredients:
1 pound ground lamb
4 ounces ground chicken
1½ tablespoons cilantro, finely chopped
1 tablespoon mint, finely chopped
1 teaspoon cumin powder
1 teaspoon coriander powder
1 teaspoon cayenne pepper powder
1 teaspoon red chili paste
2 garlic cloves, finely chopped
¼ cup olive oil
1 teaspoon salt
1 egg white

Directions:
1. Preheat air fryer to 390 degrees F.
2. Add lamb, chicken, cilantro, mint, cumin, coriander, cayenne, red chili, and garlic to a bowl and mix until well combined.
3. Add egg whites to a bowl along with salt and mix well. Pour this into meat mixture and combine into dough.
4. Roll out small balls from mixture.
5. Apply some oil on surface of meatballs and place in the basket.
6. Lower heat to 360 degrees F and cook meatballs for 6 to 8 minutes or until golden on all sides.
7. Serve with mint chutney.

Cajun Shrimp

Yield: 2 servings
Preparation Time: 5 minutes
Cooking Time: 5 minutes
Total Time: 10 minutes
Ingredients:
16 large shrimp, peeled and deveined
1 tablespoon celery salt
¼ teaspoon cayenne pepper
¼ teaspoon paprika
Dash of dry mustard
Dash of cinnamon
Salt and pepper to taste
1 tablespoon olive oil

Directions:
1. Preheat air fryer to 380 degrees F.
2. In a bowl, mix all of the spices and the oil.
3. Coat the shrimp thoroughly with the spice mix.
4. Cook the shrimp for 5 minutes.
5. Serve with rice.

Turkey Breast with Savory Glaze

Yield: 4–6 servings
Preparation Time: 10 minutes
Cooking Time: 54 minutes
Total Time: 64 minutes
Ingredients:
4–5 lbs. turkey breast
2 teaspoons olive oil
1 teaspoon thyme
½ teaspoon sage
Salt and pepper to taste
¼ cup maple syrup
2 tablespoons Dijon mustard
1 tablespoon softened butter

Directions:
1. Preheat the air fryer to 350 degrees F.
2. Coat the entire turkey breast with the olive oil.
3. Combine the spices and coat the turkey breast with the mix.
4. Place the turkey breast into the air fryer. Cook for 25 minutes.
5. Turn the turkey breast to its side and cook for 12 minutes.
6. Turn to the other side and cook for another 12 minutes.
7. For the glaze, combine the syrup, mustard, and butter.
8. Reset the turkey breast to its original position and brush on the glaze.
9. Cook for another 5 minutes.
10. Let turkey rest 10 minutes before serving.

Beef Empanadas

Yield: 4 servings
Preparation Time: 15 minutes
Cooking Time: 10 minutes
Total Time: 25 minutes
Ingredients:
1 lb. ground beef
1 onion, diced
2 garlic cloves, minced
½ bell pepper, diced
¼ cup salsa
¼ teaspoon cumin
¼ cup milk
1 egg yolk
4 empanada shells
Salt and pepper to taste

Directions:
1. Brown the ground beef, onion, and garlic in a skillet for 8 minutes.
2. Drain any excess fat and add the bell pepper, salsa, and cumin.
3. Continue browning for 5 minutes.
4. Whisk the milk and egg yolk to make an egg wash.
5. Lay out the empanada shells on a counter.
6. Fill with the meat and fold the dough over.
7. Preheat the air fryer to 350 degrees F.
8. Brush the empanadas with the egg wash and place into air fryer.
9. Cook for 10 minutes.

Beef & Broccoli

Yield: 4 servings
Preparation Time: 15 minutes
Cooking Time: 10 minutes
Total Time: 25 minutes
Ingredients:
¾ lb. round steak
1/3 cup oyster sauce
¼ cup sherry
2 tablespoon sesame oil
1 tablespoon soy sauce
1 tablespoon sugar
1 tablespoon cornstarch
1 lb. broccoli (use only the florets)
1 garlic clove, minced
1 tablespoon minced ginger
1 tablespoon olive oil

Directions:
1. Cut the steak into thin strips.
2. In a bowl, blend the oyster sauce, sherry, sesame oil, soy sauce, sugar, and cornstarch.
3. Marinate beef strips in the mixture for 1 hour.
4. Preheat air fryer to 360 degrees F.
5. Place the marinated beef, broccoli, garlic, and ginger in the air fryer.
6. Drizzle with the olive oil and cook for 12 minutes.
7. Serve over rice.

CHAPTER SEVEN

Air Fryer Dessert Recipes

Chocolate Soufflés

Yield: 4 servings
Preparation Time: 10 minutes
Cooking Time: 14 minutes
Total Time: 24 minutes
Ingredients:
3 oz. semi-sweet chocolate, chopped
¼ cup butter, plus 2 teaspoons for the ramekins
2 large eggs, separated
4 tablespoons sugar
½ teaspoon vanilla
2 tablespoons flour
Powdered sugar for dusting
Heavy cream

Directions:
1. Butter two ramekins and sprinkle with sugar.
2. Using a double boiler or a microwave, melt the chocolate with the ¼ cup butter.
3. In a bowl, whisk the eggs yolks, sugar, and vanilla.
4. Very slowly, add the melted chocolate mixture while stirring.
5. Add the flour and stir until the batter is smooth.
6. Preheat the air fryer to 330 degrees F.
7. In another bowl, beat the egg whites to a peak and gently fold into the batter.
8. Divide the batter between the prepared ramekins. Leave a bit of room on top.

9. Transfer the ramekins to the air fryer and cook for 14 minutes.

10. Remove the soufflés from the air fryer, dust with the powdered sugar and serve hot with the heavy cream.

Cinnamon Rolls

Yield: 8 servings
Preparation Time: 2 hours
Cooking Time: 20 minutes
Total Time: 2 hours 20 minutes
Ingredients:
1 lb. bread dough
¼ cup butter, melted
1 cup brown sugar
1½ tablespoons cinnamon

For the cream cheese frosting:
4 oz. cream cheese, softened
2 tablespoons softened butter
1 cup powdered sugar
½ teaspoon vanilla

Directions:
1. If the dough is frozen, thaw to room temperature.
2. On a floured surface, roll out the dough into a rectangle.
3. Brush the dough with the melted butter.
4. Combine the brown sugar and cinnamon in a small bowl.
5. Spoon the sugar mixture over the dough.
6. Roll the dough tightly into a log.
7. Press on the edges to seal the dough.
8. Cut the dough into 8 pieces.
9. Cover with a towel and let sit for 2 hours.
10. To prepare the frosting, soften the cream cheese and the butter in the microwave and stir.

11. Mix in the powdered sugar and the vanilla, and set aside.

12. Preheat the air fryer to 350 degrees F.

13. Place half of the rolls in the air fryer basket and fry for 5 minutes. Flip the rolls over and fry for 4 more minutes. Repeat with the remaining rolls.

14. Allow the rolls to cool.

15. Top with the frosting and serve warm.

Chocolate Brownies with Caramel Sauce

Yield: 6 servings
Preparation Time: 10 minutes
Cooking Time: 15 minutes
Total Time: 25 minutes
Ingredients:
4 tablespoons unsalted butter
8 oz. semi-sweet chocolate
2 large eggs
1 cup powdered sugar
¾ cup sugar
½ teaspoon salt
1 cup baking flour
1 teaspoon vanilla

Directions:
1. Preheat the air fryer to 350 degrees F.

2. Using a microwave or double boiler, melt 2 tablespoons of the butter with the chocolate.

3. Mix in the sugar, eggs, and vanilla and blend well.

4. Add the flour and mix thoroughly.

5. Transfer the mixture into a baking dish and place into the air fryer. Cook for 15 minutes.

6. For the caramel sauce, blend the powdered sugar with 1½ tablespoons water in a small pan. Let the sugar melt over medium-low heat.

7. Remove the sauce from the stove and mix in the remaining 2 tablespoons butter.

8. When the butter is melted, stir in the milk. Let cool.

9. Remove the brownies from the air fryer. Once cooled, cut them into squares and serve with the caramel sauce.

Glazed Donuts

Yield: 4 servings
Preparation Time: 5 minutes
Cooking Time: 5 minutes
Total Time: 10 minutes
Ingredients:
2 cans prepared biscuit dough
¼ cup milk
2 cups powdered sugar

Directions:
1. Preheat the air fryer to 390 degrees F.
2. For the glaze, combine the milk and the sugar. Let the sugar dissolve and set aside.
3. Use a cookie cutter or shot glass to poke a hole in the biscuit.
4. Spray the bottom of the air fryer with non-stick cooking spray and insert the donuts.
5. Air fry for 5 minutes.
6. Remove the donuts from the air fryer, and drop each donut in the glaze.
7. Let sit for a few minutes. Add sprinkles if desired.

Carrot Cake

Yield: 6 servings
Preparation Time: 15 minutes
Cooking Time: 30 minutes
Total Time: 45 minutes
Ingredients:
2 cups flour

2 teaspoons baking soda

1 teaspoon cinnamon

½ teaspoon salt

½ cup honey

½ cup canola oil

½ cup applesauce

¼ cup plain yogurt

3 large eggs

2 teaspoons vanilla

2 carrots, shredded

½ cup raisins

½ cup walnuts

For the Frosting:
1 cup cream cheese, softened

1 cup powdered sugar

½ cup plain yogurt

1 teaspoon vanilla

1 teaspoon lemon juice

¼ teaspoon milk ONLY if needed to soften icing.

Directions:
1. Spray the baking tray with a non-stick cooking spray.

2. In a bowl, sift together the flour, baking soda, cinnamon, and salt. Set aside.

3. In a mixer with a bowl, whip together the honey and the oil. Add the applesauce and the yogurt.

4. Add 1 egg at a time, whipping the mixture well after each egg. Add the vanilla.

5. Preheat the air fryer to 350 degrees F.

6. Use a spatula to blend the wet ingredients into the dry mixture.

7. Gently mix in the shredded carrots, raisins, and walnuts.

8. Pour the batter into the baking tray and place in the air fryer. Cover the tray with foil.

9. Bake for 30 minutes.

10. Remove the carrot cake and let cool.

11. For the frosting, use a food processer to soften the cream cheese.

12. Add the powdered sugar and blend until smooth.

13. Add the yogurt, vanilla, and lemon juice and blend further. Let the frosting thicken in the refrigerator for a few hours.

14. Frost the carrot cake and top with walnuts.

Chocolate Cake

Yield: 6 servings
Preparation Time: 15 minutes
Cooking Time: 25 minutes
Total Time: 40 minutes
Ingredients:
3 large eggs
1 stick butter, softened
1 cup flour
2/3 cup sugar
½ cup sour cream
1/3 cup cocoa powder
2 teaspoons vanilla
1 teaspoon baking powder
½ teaspoon baking soda

For the Chocolate Frosting:
2 cups powdered sugar
½ cup butter, softened
3 tablespoons cocoa powder
2 tablespoons heavy cream
⅛ teaspoon salt

Directions:
1. Preheat air fryer to 320 degrees F.
2. Combine all the ingredients in a mixing bowl until smooth.
3. Pour the batter into a baking dish and place into the air fryer.
4. Bake for 25 minutes. Insert toothpick to test for doneness. Bake for 5 more minutes, if needed and allow cake to cool.
5. For the frosting, mix the sugar, butter, cocoa powder, cream, and salt until smooth.
6. Frost the cake and serve.

Chocolate Chip Cookies

Yield: 9 servings
Preparation Time: 5 minutes
Cooking Time: 8 minutes
Total Time: 13 minutes
Ingredients:
4 oz. butter
3 oz. brown sugar
2 tablespoons honey
¾ cup flour
¾ cup chocolate
1½ tablespoons milk

Directions:
1. Preheat the air fryer to 360 degrees F.
2. Cream the butter and sugar until smooth.
3. Add the honey and stir; add the flour and continue stirring.
4. Use a mallet or rolling pin to break the chocolate into chunks.
5. Mix the chocolate and milk into the batter and blend well.
6. Place a baking sheet in the air fryer, and spoon the batter into the air fryer making 9 cookies.
7. Bake for 6 minutes. Reduce heat to 340 degrees F and bake another 2 minutes or until light brown.

Banana Cake

Yield: 9 servings
Preparation Time: 5 minutes
Cooking Time: 8 minutes
Total Time: 13 minutes
Ingredients:
½ cup butter, softened
½ cup sugar
2 large eggs
2 large bananas, mashed
1¼ cups baking flour
2 tablespoons buttermilk
½ teaspoon baking soda
⅛ teaspoon salt

Directions:
1. Cream the butter and sugar with an electric mixer.
2. Continue mixing, adding one egg at a time, then stir in the bananas.
3. Mix in the remaining ingredients.
4. Preheat the air fryer at 350 degrees F.
5. Butter a baking pan and drizzle it with flour.
6. Pour the batter into the baking pan.
7. Place the baking pan in the air fryer and cook for 35 minutes.
8. Insert a toothpick in center of cake to check for doneness.
9. Let cool and serve.

Conclusion

The air fryer is a revolutionary kitchen appliance. This book provides you with easy and delicious air fryer recipes you can whip up in minutes—even if you don't know how to cook.

I hope you enjoy the recipes!

Finally, I want to thank you for reading my book. If you enjoyed the book, please take the time to share your thoughts and post a review on the book retailer's website. It would be greatly appreciated!

Best wishes,
Savannah Gibbs

Check Out My Other Books

Fermentation for Beginners: Delicious Fermented Vegetable Recipes for Better Digestion and Health

Mediterranean Diet Cookbook: Easy and Delicious Mediterranean Diet Recipes to Lose Weight and Lower Your Risk of Heart Disease